gǒu mā ma yù jiàn jī mā ma
狗妈妈遇见鸡妈妈

Mother Dog Met Mother Hen

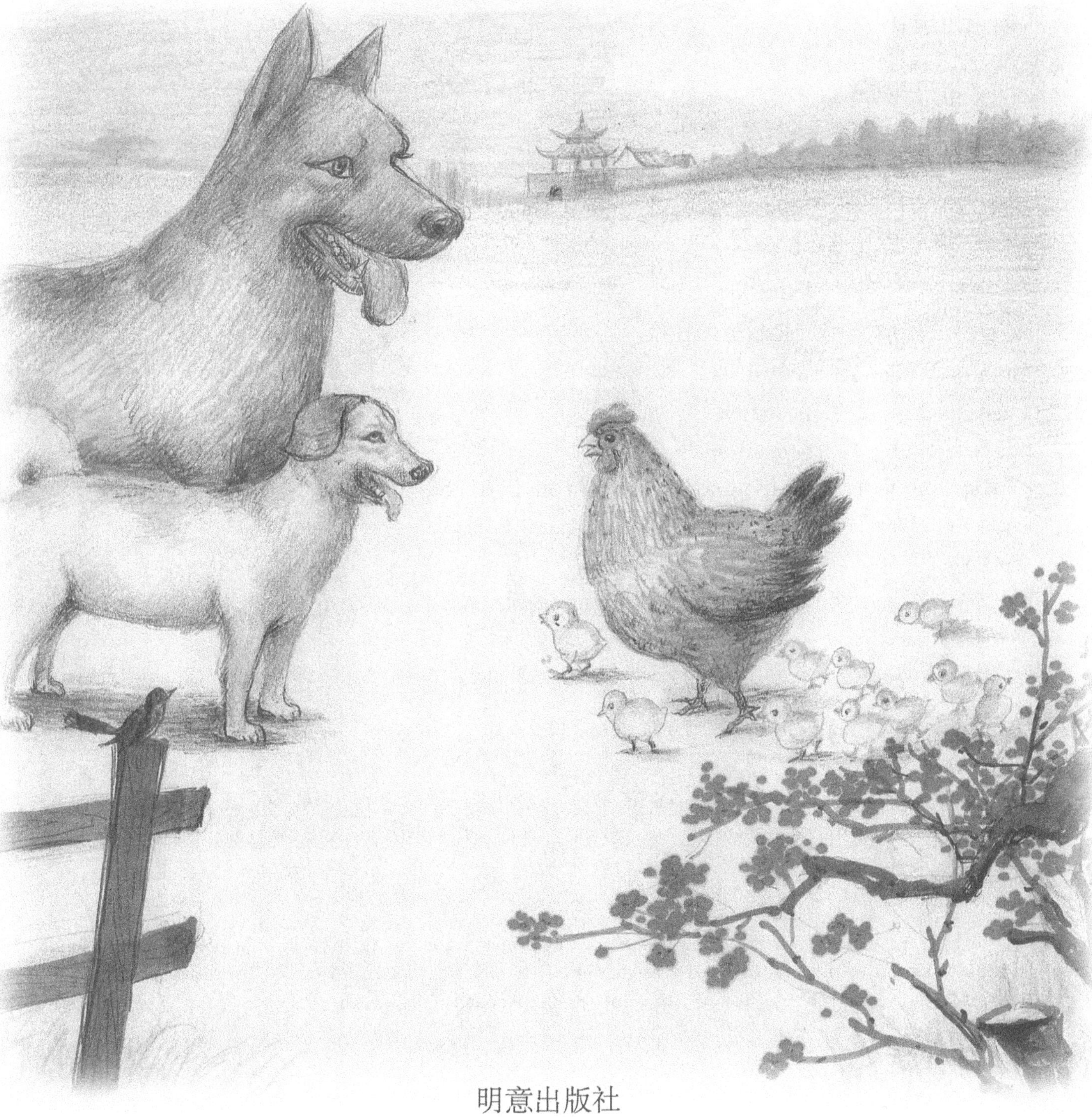

明意出版社
Ming Yi Chinese Publication Limited

狗妈妈遇见鸡妈妈

作者：卢月云
插图：戴益
编辑：明意编辑组
出版：明意出版社
电子邮件：mingyipub@gmail.com（mingyichinese.com）
脸书：http://on.fb.me/1Ju8fh4
设计：Papercome Limited（www.papercome.co.uk）

©明意出版社
二零一五年四月初版　版权所有

在未经出版者书面许可的情况下，本书的任何部分不得以任何方式，无论是电子或机械形式，包括影印、录音，或透过任何信息检索系统来复制或传送。

国际标准书号978-0-9930499-2-7

在编写本书时已尽力采取措施防止错误或遗漏，出版者和作者对其中的错误或遗漏概不负责，也不承担因使用此书中的任何內容引致的损失的任何责任。

Mother Dog Met Mother Hen

Author : Yuet-wan Lo
Illustrator : David Dai
Editor : Ming Yi Editorial Team
Published by Ming Yi Chinese Publication Limited
For more information, email : mingyipub@gmail.com (mingyichinese.com)
Facebook : http://on.fb.me/1Ju8fh4
Designed by Papercome Limited　(www.papercome.co.uk)

First edition published in the United Kingdom in April 2015

Copyright © 2015 Ming Yi Chinese Publication Limited. All rights reserved.

No part of this book shall be reproduced or transmitted in any form or by any means, electronic or mechanical, including photocopying, recording, or by any information retrieval system without written permission of the publisher.

ISBN 978-0-9930499-2-7

Although every precaution has been taken in the preparation of this book, the publisher and author assume no responsibility for errors or omissions. Neither is any liability assumed for damages resulting from the use of this information contained herein.

作者及插图师简介
Introduction of the Author and Illustrator

卢月云 Yuet-wan Lo（作者 Author）

原居于香港，毕业于香港中文大学，于1996年移居英国。她在香港时任教中文和社会科学科十年，业余从事文学创作，在多项的文学创作比赛中获奖，包括1990年的新雅文化出版社第六届文学创作比赛(儿童故事组)亚军及华侨日报六十五周年报庆创作比赛(妇女散文组)亚军，并于1994至1995年间获得其他创作比赛的优异奖。著有《耶稣在校园》和《从眼泪到欢笑》两书。现职为英国的专业翻译和传译员。

Yuet-wan Lo originates from Hong Kong. She graduated from the Chinese University of Hong Kong and later moved to the United Kingdom in 1996. She taught Chinese and Social Science subjects in schools in Hong Kong for 10 years. During this time, she started writing for publication and won several awards in writing competitions in Hong Kong, including the first runner-up in The Sixth Creative Writing Competition (Children Story) by Sun Ya Publications Limited and the 65th Anniversary Writing Competition (Women's Group-Essay) by Wah Kiu Daily News in 1990. She also won a few writing merit awards in 1994 and 1995. She is the author of two books titled Jesus Works in the Campus (2001) and From Tears to Laughter (2014). She currently works as a professional translator and interpreter in the U.K.

戴益 Yi Dai（插图师 Illustrator）

原居中国四川重庆，于1994年移居英国。毕业于四川美术学院，主修油画，选修中国国画，获颁赠美术学士学位，于国内外教授画班二十年。他於2015年完成国际欧华神学院的神学硕士课程。现职为教会传道人。

David Dai originates from Sichuan, Chongqing. He moved to the United Kingdom in 1994. He completed the Oil Painting (major) and Chinese Painting courses in Sichuan Fine Arts Institute and was awarded a Bachelor's Degree in Fine Art. He has been teaching painting classes for 20 years. In 2015, he graduated from International Chinese Biblical Seminary in Europe with a Master's Degree in Theology. He is now serving in a church as a pastoral worker.

如何使用本书帮助儿童学习中文

本书的目的：
培养儿童阅读 简体中文的兴趣。
通过有趣的动物图画故事，辅助儿童学习普通话。

本书阅读对象：
本书以简体中文书写，文字上面注有普通话拼音，在每页的下面印有故事的英文翻译。
学习普通话三年或以上的儿童可独立阅读本书，学习普通话三年以下的儿童，建议家长或老师辅助阅读。

家长或老师使用本书辅助儿童阅读的建议：
在本书的第48页有供家长或老师使用帮助儿童学习字词的"重点学习：中、英文名词、动词和形容词表"（附英文翻译）。与儿童一起阅读前，请先看此页，以掌握儿童通过这个故事可以学到的名词、动词和形容词。

以生动的音调用普通话阅读这个故事给儿童听，在阅读故事时，一面讲，一面指着插图中对应的人物、动物或物件引起他们对故事的兴趣，帮助他们理解内容。

当读到拟声词时，要着意模仿那声音，增加儿童阅读的兴趣；当读到动词或形容词时，可以做出表情或动作，让孩子能更加理解词义。

若儿童的母语为英语而又不明白普通话的故事内容，你可以用每页中的英文翻译辅助说明。

在第46页和第47页有两个动脑筋活动，以增加儿童阅读的趣味并鼓励他们重温故事。请家长、老师或助教鼓励儿童完成这两页，使学习更有效。你可在第49页找到答案。

第50页印有汉语拼音基本音素和四声表，若要得到更多的指引和例子，请到我们的网站参考 (mingyichinese.com)。

以上只是本社编辑组给家长、老师或助教的参考意见，帮助儿童阅读时，应按着每个儿童的个别需要作考虑而使用本书。

*关于本书或本社出版的其他书籍的任何查询，请发电子邮件至明意出版社
(电子邮件地址 **mingyipub@gmail.com**)。

How to use this book to help children learn Chinese

The Aims of this Book:
To cultivate children's interest in reading Chinese.
To assist children to learn Chinese through reading an interesting illustrated animal story.

Targeted Readers:
This book is written in simplified Chinese with Mandarin Pinyin (Mandarin phonetics) on top of the Chinese writing and with English translation below. Children who have learnt Mandarin for at least three years should be able to read and understand this story by themselves. For children who have not learnt Mandarin before or have learnt Mandarin for less than three years, it is recommended that parents and teachers assist them in reading this book.

Suggestions for parents and teachers:
On Page 48, there are Tables of Nouns, Verbs and Adjectives for Learning Chinese (with English Translation). Please read this page and understand the foci of learning for this book.

When reading this book in Mandarin to your child/children, you can use a lively voice to attract their attention and enhance their interest in the story, and point to the corresponding people, animals or objects in the illustrations to help them understand the meaning of the words.

When you are reading out words which simulate the sounds of animals or movements of objects, you can also use a lively voice to attract your child/children's attention. When reading out a verb or an adjective, you can use appropriate gestures or expressions to help them understand the meaning.

If your child/children speaks/speak English as their mother tongue and does/do not fully understand the Mandarin which you read out, you can also read the English translation on each page to help them understand.

On Page 46 and Page 47, there are two activities which aim to help children recap on the story and give them some fun after the reading. The answers for the activities are printed on Page 49.

On Page 50, there is a table of Chinese Pinyin Basic Sounds and Four Tones to provide you some basic knowledge of the Pinyin pronunciations. For more guidance and examples, please visit our website mingyichinese.com.

These are only suggested guidelines from our editorial team. You should adapt these guidelines to the individual needs of your child/children.

*For any inquiries or feedback about this book or our other publications, please email us on mingyipub@gmail.com.

6

狗妈妈遇见鸡妈妈
Mother Dog Met Mother Hen

gū gū gū jī mā ma zài shēng dàn fū xiǎo jī
咕！咕！咕！鸡妈妈在生蛋孵小鸡。

xiǎo jī cóng dàn lǐ fū chū lái la
小鸡从蛋里孵出来啦！

jī jī jī xiǎo jī jiào dào
唧！唧！唧！小鸡叫道：

mā ma mā ma
"妈妈！妈妈！"

jī mā ma kāi xīn de bù tíng de gū gū jiào
鸡妈妈开心得不停地咕咕叫！

CLUCK! CLUCK! CLUCK!
Mother Hen laid some eggs.
The eggs were hatched and the chicks came out!
CHIRP! CHIRP! CHIRP! They Chirped, "Mama! Mama!"
Mother Hen was so HAPPY that she could not help CLUCKING all the time!

7

狗妈妈遇见鸡妈妈
Mother Dog Met Mother Hen

8

狗妈妈遇见鸡妈妈
Mother Dog Met Mother Hen

gǒu mā ma yù jiàn le jī mā ma
狗妈妈遇见了鸡妈妈，

wāng wāng wāng gū gū gū
汪！汪！汪！咕！咕！咕！

wāng gū wāng gū wāng wāng gū
汪咕！汪咕！汪汪咕！

xiǎo gǒu áng áng de duì xiǎo jī shuō
小狗昂昂地对小鸡说：

wǒ men mā ma de shēng yīn zhēn xiǎng liàng
"我们妈妈的声音真响亮！"

xiǎo jī jī jī de dá dào
小鸡唧唧地答道：

shì a zhēn shì xiǎng liàng a
"是啊！真是响亮啊！"

Mother Dog met Mother Hen.
WOOF! WOOF! WOOF! CLUCK! CLUCK! CLUCK!
WOOF! CLUCK! WOOF! CLUCK! WOOF! WOOF! CLUCK!
YAP! YAP! YAP! Puppy said to the chicks,
"Our mothers' voices are so LOUD!"
"Yes, they are VERY LOUD!" The chicks replied together.
 CHIRP! CHIRP! CHIRP!

狗妈妈遇见鸡妈妈
Mother Dog Met Mother Hen

10
狗妈妈遇见鸡妈妈
Mother Dog Met Mother Hen

gǒu mā ma duì jī mā ma shuō
狗妈妈对鸡妈妈说:
nǐ gāng shēng wán xiǎo jī yào duō xiū xi a
"你刚生完小鸡,要多休息啊!"
jī mā ma xiào zhe duì gǒu mā ma shuō
鸡妈妈笑着对狗妈妈说:
wǒ shēng jī dàn, rán hòu fū xiǎo jī
"我生鸡蛋,然后孵小鸡,
suǒ yǐ shì bú yòng xiū xí de
所以是不用休息的。"

Mother Dog said to Mother Hen,
"You have just given birth to your chicks.
You need to REST!"
Mother Hen smiled and said to Mother Dog,
"I lay eggs and then hatch eggs.
So I do NOT need to rest!"

狗妈妈遇见鸡妈妈
Mother Dog Met Mother Hen

12
狗妈妈遇见鸡妈妈
Mother Dog Met Mother Hen

gǒu mā ma bù xiāng xìn
狗妈妈不相信

jī mā ma zhǐ shì shēng dàn hé fū dàn
鸡妈妈只是生蛋和孵蛋，

biàn fū chū xiǎo jī lái,
便孵出小鸡来，

tā shuō wǒ bù shēng dàn, wǒ shēng xiǎo gǒu
她说："我不生蛋！我生小狗，

shēng wán zhī hòu yào xiū xi de
生完之后要休息的！"

Mother Dog did not believe that Mother Hen laid eggs and hatched eggs, and her chicks were hatched from her eggs.
She said, "I did NOT lay any egg! I gave birth to my puppy. After I had given birth, I needed to REST!"

14

狗妈妈遇见鸡妈妈

Mother Dog Met Mother Hen

狗妈妈又说：

"动物妈妈们也不生蛋，

只生她们的宝宝！

她们生完宝宝之后，

都要休息的！"

Mother Dog also said,
"ALL the other animals do NOT lay eggs.
They give birth to their babies!
After they have given birth to their babies,
they need to REST!"

16
狗妈妈遇见鸡妈妈
Mother Dog Met Mother Hen

jī mā ma shuō nǐ bú xìn
鸡妈妈说:"你不信?
wǒ men yì qǐ qù wèn niǎo mā ma
我们一起去问鸟妈妈,
tā yě zhǐ shì shēng dàn hé fū dàn
她也只是生蛋和孵蛋,
biàn fū chū xiǎo niǎo lái
便孵出小鸟来!"
gǒu mā ma dá dào
狗妈妈答道:
hǎo ba wǒ dài xiǎo gǒu yì qǐ qù
"好吧!我带小狗一起去!"

Mother Hen said,
"You do NOT believe me?
Let's go to ask Mother Bird!
She also lays eggs and hatches eggs, and
her little birds COME OUT of her eggs!"
Mother Dog replied,
"OK! I will go with Puppy!"

狗妈妈遇见鸡妈妈
Mother Dog Met Mother Hen

18

狗妈妈遇见鸡妈妈
Mother Dog Met Mother Hen

xiǎo gǒu tīng dào hòu shuō wǒ bù xiǎng qù
小狗听到后,说:"我不想去!
tiān shàng de dà niǎo hěn kě pà huì zhuā dòng wù chī de
天上的大鸟很可怕,会抓动物吃的!"
gǒu mā ma shuō nà zhǐ shì dà yīng
狗妈妈说:"那只是大鹰!"
xiǎo gǒu bù xiāng xìn biàn zì jǐ huí jiā qù le
小狗不相信,便自己回家去了。

"I am NOT going!" said Puppy when he heard this.
"Big birds in the sky are SCARY! They will catch animals to eat!"
Mother Dog said, "Those are ONLY EAGLES!"
Puppy did NOT believe it. He went home by himself.

狗妈妈遇见鸡妈妈
Mother Dog Met Mother Hen

小狗离开后，
鸡妈妈和狗妈妈
便一起去找鸟妈妈，
小鸡们也跟着去。

After Puppy had left,
Mother Hen and Mother Dog went to see Mother Bird together.
The chicks followed.

22
狗妈妈遇见鸡妈妈
Mother Dog Met Mother Hen

tā men jiàn dào niǎo mā ma
他们见到鸟妈妈，
biàn hù xiāng wèn hǎo
便互相问好。
wāng wāng wāng gū gū gū
汪！汪！汪！咕！咕！咕！
zhā zhā zhā
喳！喳！喳！

When they saw Mother Bird,
they greeted each other.
WOOF! WOOF! WOOF!
CLUCK! CLUCK! CLUCK!
TWEET! TWEET! TWEET!

狗妈妈遇见鸡妈妈
Mother Dog Met Mother Hen

24
狗妈妈遇见鸡妈妈
Mother Dog Met Mother Hen

狗妈妈问鸟妈妈:
"你生蛋吗?
你的小鸟是从蛋里孵出来的吗?"
鸟妈妈答道:
"是啊,我生蛋,我孵蛋,
我的小鸟是从蛋里孵出来的!"

Mother Dog asked Mother Bird,
"Do you lay eggs?
Are your little birds hatched from your eggs?"
Mother Bird replied,
"Yes, I LAY my eggs. I HATCH my eggs.
My little birds are hatched from my eggs!"

狗妈妈遇见鸡妈妈
Mother Dog Met Mother Hen

26
狗妈妈遇见鸡妈妈
Mother Dog Met Mother Hen

狗妈妈仍然不相信。
鸟妈妈又喳喳地说：
"你看，这是我的鸟蛋！"
狗妈妈说：
"不是啊，这些只是小卵石！"
汪！汪！汪！

Mother Dog still did not believe it.
Then Mother Bird said,
"LOOK, these are my EGGS!"
TWEET! TWEET! TWEET!
Mother Dog said,
"NO! These are ONLY small PEBBLES!"
WOOF! WOOF! WOOF!

狗妈妈遇见鸡妈妈
Mother Dog Met Mother Hen

niǎo mā ma shēng qì de shuō
鸟妈妈生气地说:
"niǎo ér shēng dàn niǎo ér fū dàn
鸟儿生蛋,鸟儿孵蛋!
xiǎo niǎo shì cóng dàn lǐ fū chū lái de
小鸟是从蛋里孵出来的!"

Mother Bird said angrily,
"Birds LAY EGGS. Birds HATCH EGGS.
Little birds are HATCHED from the EGGS!"

30
狗妈妈遇见鸡妈妈
Mother Dog Met Mother Hen

gǒu mā ma hái shì bù xiāng xìn
狗妈妈还是不相信，
jī mā ma yě shēng qì le
鸡妈妈也生气了，
gū gū gū
咕！咕！咕！
tā dài zhe xiǎo jī huí jiā qù le
她带着小鸡回家去了。
jī jī jī
唧！唧！唧！

Mother Dog still did not believe it.
Mother Hen was VERY UPSET!
CLUCK! CLUCK! CLUCK!
She went home with her chicks.
CHIRP! CHIRP! CHIRP!

31

狗妈妈遇见鸡妈妈
Mother Dog Met Mother Hen

狗妈妈遇见鸡妈妈
Mother Dog Met Mother Hen

有一天，狗妈妈带小狗出来玩。
汪！汪！汪！昂！昂！昂！

One day, Mother Dog took Puppy to the woodland to play.
WOOF! WOOF! WOOF! YAP! YAP! YAP!

狗妈妈遇见鸡妈妈
Mother Dog Met Mother Hen

34

狗妈妈遇见鸡妈妈
Mother Dog Met Mother Hen

tā men kàn iàn
他们看见
zài shù xià yǒu yì zhǐ dà yīng dàn
在树下有一只大鹰蛋，
què yǐ wéi nà shì yí kuài dà luǎn shí
却以为那是一块大卵石！

They saw a LARGE eagle egg under a tree
but they thought that it was a LARGE PEBBLE!

狗妈妈遇见鸡妈妈
Mother Dog Met Mother Hen

36

狗妈妈遇见鸡妈妈

Mother Dog Met Mother Hen

xiǎo gǒu pā zài nà zhǐ dà yīng dàn shàng
小 狗 趴 在 那 只 大 鹰 蛋 上

xiū xi yí xià
休 息 一 下,

hū hū hū hū shuì zháo le
呼 呼… 呼 呼..睡 着 了!

tā de shēn tǐ nuǎn huo zhe nà zhǐ dà yīng dàn
他 的 身 体 暖 和 着 那 只 大 鹰 蛋!

Puppy lay on the large eagle egg for a rest.
Zzz… Zzz… He FELL ASLEEP!
His body gave warm to the large eagle egg!

狗妈妈遇见鸡妈妈
Mother Dog Met Mother Hen

狗妈妈遇见鸡妈妈
Mother Dog Met Mother Hen

dà yīng dàn liè kāi pī pāi pī pāi
大鹰蛋裂开，噼啪！噼啪！

xiǎo gǒu pā zài dì shàng kàn
小狗趴在地上看…

à cóng nà zhī dà yīng dàn jìng rán fū chū le
啊！从那只大鹰蛋竟然孵出了

yì zhī xiǎo yīng lái
一只小鹰来！

dàn tā men réng rán bù xiāng xìn
但他们仍然不相信

niǎo shì cóng dàn li fū chū lái de
鸟是从蛋里孵出来的！

The large eagle egg CRACKED! Crack! Crack! Crack!
Puppy was lying on the ground watching…
Oh! A small eagle was ACTUALLY hatched
from the large eagle egg!
But they still did NOT believe that
birds are ACTUALLY hatched from the eggs!

狗妈妈遇见鸡妈妈
Mother Dog Met Mother Hen

40

狗妈妈遇见鸡妈妈
Mother Dog Met Mother Hen

áng áng　áng áng　áng áng áng
昂昂！昂昂！昂昂昂！
xiǎo gǒu fēi cháng hài pà dà jiào
小狗非常害怕，大叫：
yǒu guài shòu a
"有怪兽啊！"

YAP YAP! YAP YAP! YAP YAP YAP!
Puppy was VERY SCARED and shouted,
"ARGH! ARGH! There is a MONSTER!"

42
狗妈妈遇见鸡妈妈
Mother Dog Met Mother Hen

汪汪！汪汪！汪汪汪！
狗妈妈也非常害怕，大叫：
"有怪兽啊！"

WOOF WOOF! WOOF WOOF! WOOF WOOF WOOF!
Mother Dog was also VERY SCARED and shouted,
"ARGH! ARGH! There is a MONSTER!"

44

狗妈妈遇见鸡妈妈

Mother Dog Met Mother Hen

汪！汪！汪！昂！昂！昂！
汪！昂！汪！昂！汪！昂！昂！
狗妈妈和小狗吓得一起跑回家！

WOOF! WOOF! WOOF! YAP! YAP! YAP!
WOOF! YAP! WOOF! YAP! WOOF! YAP! YAP!
Mother Dog and Puppy were so SCARED that they DASHED home together!

狗妈妈遇见鸡妈妈
Mother Dog Met Mother Hen

动脑筋活动 Activity 1:

从下面右列选出图片中动物或物件的中文名称，并且参看拼音读出名称。

Choose a Chinese name from the right column below for each of the animals or objects in the pictures and say the name with the help of the Pinyin.

动物和物件
Animal and Object

中文名称
Chinese Name

●   ● jī mā ma
鸡 妈 妈

●   ● yīng dàn
鹰 蛋

●   ● xiǎo gǒu
小 狗

●   ● xiǎo jī
小 鸡

●   ● gǒu mā ma
狗 妈 妈

●   ● niǎo mā ma
鸟 妈 妈

狗妈妈遇见鸡妈妈
Mother Dog Met Mother Hen

动脑筋活动 Activity 2:
从下面选出句子描述每一幅故事图片中发生的事。

Choose the sentences from below to describe what happened in each of the pictures.

1. 狗妈妈说, 鸡妈妈刚生完小鸡要休息。Mother Dog said that Mother Hen needed to rest after she had given birth.
2. 鸡妈妈说, 她生旦孵小鸡, 是不用休息的。Mother Hen said that she laid and hatched eggs so she did not need to rest.
3. 鸟妈妈也说, 她是生旦孵小鸟的。 Mother Bird said that she also laid eggs and hatched her little birds.
4. 狗妈妈和小狗以为大鹰旦是大卵石。Mother Dog and Puppy thought that the large eagle egg was a large pebble.
5. 小狗趴在那只大鹰旦上, 后来孵出了小鹰来。Puppy lay on the large eagle egg, later a small eagle was hatched.
6. 狗妈妈和小狗以为小鹰是怪兽, 吓得跑回家!
Mother Dog and Puppy thought that the small eagle was a monster. They were so scared that they dashed home!

*请到第49页查看你的答案是否正确。Please turn to Page 49 to check your answers.

47

狗妈妈遇见鸡妈妈
Mother Dog Met Mother Hen

重点学习：中、英文名词、动词和形容词表（附英文翻译）
Tables of Important Nouns, Verbs and Adjectives for Learning Chinese (with English Translations)

表一：名词 Table One: Nouns

简体中文	普通话拼音	英文翻译
鸡	jī	hen
妈妈	mā ma	mother
蛋	dàn	egg
小鸡	xiǎo jī	chick
狗	gǒu	dog
小狗	xiǎo gǒu	puppy
宝宝	bǎo bao	baby
鹰	yīng	eagle
卵石	luǎn shí	pebble
怪兽	guài shòu	monster

表二：动词表 Table 2: Verbs

简体中文	普通话拼音	英文翻译
生	shēng	give birth
孵	fū	hatch
出来	chū lái	come out
遇见	yù jiàn	meet
看见	kàn jiàn	see
说	shuō	say
相信	xiāng xìn	believe
趴	pā	lie
睡着	shuì zháo	fall asleep
裂开	liè kāi	crack
跑	pǎo	run
问	wèn	ask
答	dá	reply
回	huí	go back

表三：形容词 Table 3: Adjectives

简体中文	普通话拼音	英文翻译
大	dà	large
害怕	hài pà	scared

狗妈妈遇见鸡妈妈
Mother Dog Met Mother Hen

动脑筋活动一答案 Answers for Activity 1:

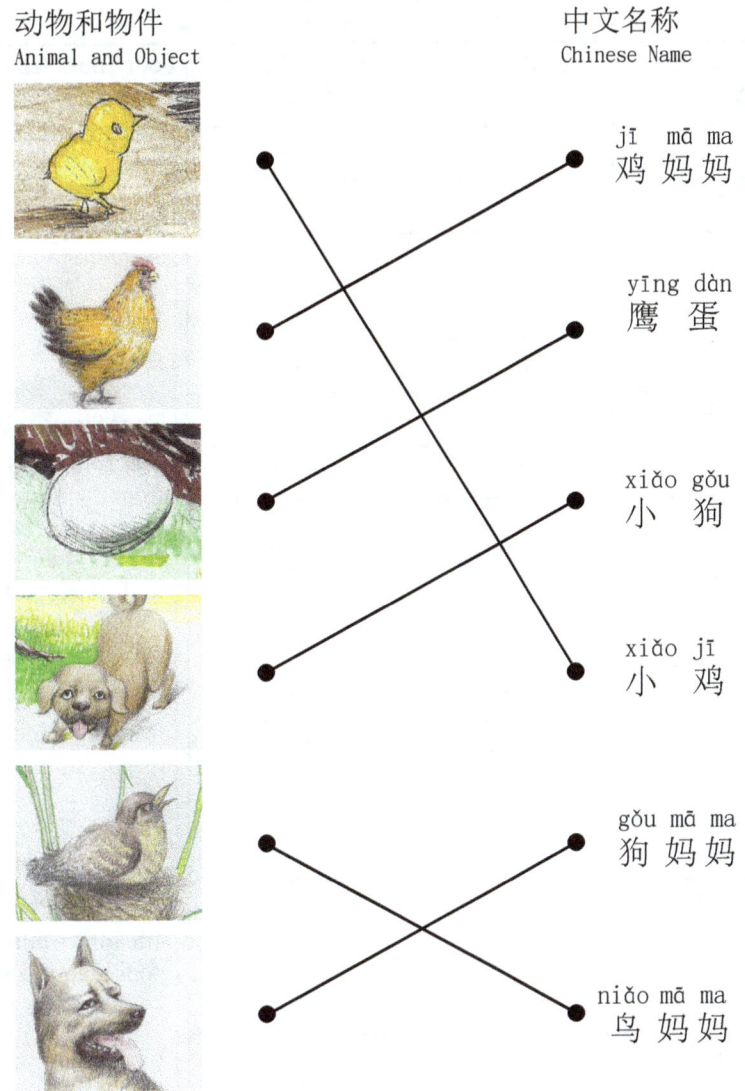

动脑筋活动二答案 Answers for Activity 2:

Chinese Pinyin Basic Sounds and Four Tones
汉语拼音基本音素及四声

Initial Symbol 始音标	Initial Sound 起始音	Final Symbol 尾音标	Final Sound 结尾音	Four Tones (shown by the sign above the Pinyin) 四声（在拼音上的符号表示）
b	baw	a	ah	1st Tone - High Level: high pitched and hold the sound there slightly longer than seems natural, e.g. first sound in "mother", m ā ma (m ā) 第一声：高音调 以高音调发音，比一般说话时持续稍长一点时间，例如："妈妈"（m ā ma）中的第一个"妈"（m ā）。 Tone Sign 声调符号（ ˉ ）
p	paw	ai	i	
m	maw	ao	ow	
f	faw	an	ahn	
d	duh	ang	ahng	
t	tuh	o	aw	
n	nuh	ong	oong	2nd Tone - Rising: from the middle level of your voice range to the top, e.g. hemp (m á) 第二声：向上转为高音调 由中音调开始向上转为高音调，例如："麻"（m á）。 Tone Sign 声调符号（ ´ ）
l	luh	ou	oh	
g	guh	e	uh	
k	kuh	ei	ay	
h	huh	en	un	3rd Tone - Falling And Then Rising: from the middle level, go down deep, then rise up a bit, e.g. horse (m ǎ). 第三声：变为低音，再转为高音调 以中音调开始，然后变为低音，再转为高音调，例如："马"（m ǎ）。 Tone Sign 声调符号（ ˇ ）
j	gee	eng	ung	
q	chee	er	ar	
x	she	i	ee/uh	
z	dzuh	ia	ya	
c	tsuh	iao	yaow	4th Tone - falling: a short, sharp fall from your high voice pitch. Stress the sound in your voice as you say it, e.g. scold (m à). 第四声：急速变为低音调：高音调开始，短而急速变为低音，说时要加重声线，例如："骂"（m à）。 Tone Sign 声调符号（ ˋ ）
s	suh	ian	yan	
zh	jir	iang	yahng	
ch	chir	ie	yeh	
sh	shir	in	een	* The light way of saying a word - The four tones represent different ways of emphasizing the sound of a word. Sometimes we say a word in a light way without any emphasis. If you see a word without any Pinyin tonation symbol above it, it means that you should say it in a light way, e.g. the second sound in "mother" (mā ma). 轻声：上面的四声是不同的发音音调，汉语发音中有完全不强调任何音节，只轻轻说出一个字，是为轻声。例子如"妈妈"中的第二个"妈"字（ma）。 No Tone Sign 不加符号
r	rj	ing	eeng	
w	ooh	iong	yoong	
y	ee	iu	you	
		u	oo	
		ua	wa	
		uo	waw	
		ui	way	
		uai	why	
		uan	won	
		un	un	Reference 参考书籍: Elinor Greenwood, "Easy Peasy Chinese - Mandarin Chinese for Beginners", Dorling Kindersley Limited, 2007, London.
		uang	wahng	
		ü	yoo	
		ue	oo-weh	* For more guidance and reference, please visit our webiste. (mingyichinese.com)
		üan	ywan	
		ün	yewn	

www.ingramcontent.com/pod-product-compliance
Lightning Source LLC
Chambersburg PA
CBHW080811010526
44113CB00013B/2366